Bipolar

Creating The Right Bipolar Diet & Nutritional Plan to Deal with Bipolar Type II Today

By: Samantha Rose

Have You Read My Book?
Please Leave Your Comments Now!
I Appreciate It Very Much
http://www.amazon.com/dp/B008A8TRHG

Other Kindle Books In the Bipolar Series

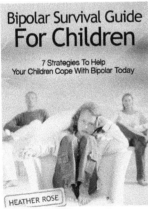

Other Kindle Books In The Bipolar Series

Other books by Heather Rose

Please visit my author page now

http://amazon.com/author/ultimatesurvivorguides

Table of Contents

Introduction

You may not know this but Bipolar Type 2 is one of the most common mental disorders, which people suffer from these days. Due to symptoms being less severe, many refer to it as "soft bipolar". Yet, even though the symptoms associated with type 2 are less intense, it can still have a detrimental effect on the quality of life for the sufferer.

In fact, they often find it extremely troubling as they have the classic symptoms of bipolar type 1. They can be subject to serious and recurring bouts of depression, along with more subtle bipolar symptoms such as periods of irritability, confusion, impulsiveness and agitation.

When bipolar type 2 sufferers have a manic episode, it is usually milder so rather than being hyperactive, they tend to feel more energized and happier. Due to this, they do not suffer the terrible repercussions of a full-blown manic episode.

However, it is worth saying that even though the symptoms are less severe they still need the right course of medication and therapy so they are able to take control of their illness. If they do not, then there is a chance their condition can become worse, which could have serious consequences.

Unfortunately studies show that bipolar type 2 has become much more prevalent. In fact, it is now believed bipolar type 2 is three to four times more common than bipolar type 1. Yet, no one can offer an explanation as to why this has become the case. However, it could be because bipolar disorder was categorized into four different classifications, therefore has now become much easier to recognize and diagnose.

Even though it has become more prevalent, many believe patients are receiving the wrong diagnosis. Many say the reason for this is that the manic episodes in bipolar type 2 are much less severe than those of type 1,so can class as being in a "normal" state of elation.

Furthermore, if the symptoms associated with hypomania manifest themselves as racing thoughts, anxiety, insomnia or irritability then it becomes difficult for medical professionals to determine whether they suffer from bipolar type 2 or depression. Often when a person suffers a manic episode they usually feel elated but for those who are bipolar type two, they usually feel more depressed rather than elation.

Bipolar type 2 sufferers also experience "mixed episodes". These are the kind of episodes where they have symptoms associated with hypomania and depression at the same time. As a result, their moods will change much more often, which could be within a matter of hours or days.

Rapid cycling is also another symptom of bipolar type 2. To class as suffering from this, a person needs to have experienced at least four changes in mood state in any given year.

If you are at all concerned you may be suffering from bipolar type 2, do not hesitate to see your doctor and seek advice. Never put off doing this as your condition could become worse. The sooner you find out if you have bipolar type 2 the sooner, you can start treatment.

Chapter 1
What is Bipolar Type 2 Disorder?

Bipolar type 2 is a form of mental illness similar to that of bipolar type 1. Just like bipolar 1, type 2 sufferers experience episodes of highs and lows over a period of time.

However, the major difference is, when a bipolar 2 suffers a manic episode it doesn't reach full on mania. This less severe mania is termed "hypomania" or "hypomanic".

For those been diagnosed as having bipolar type 2 will know that to have been diagnosed as such they have to experience at least one episode of hypomania in their life. Saying that, type 2 sufferers tend to experience more depressive episodes than manic ones, which is where the term "manic depression" comes from.

Generally, anyone suffering from this condition will find that between their hypomania and depressive episodes they are able to lead relatively normal lives.

Characteristics of Bipolar Type 2 Hypomanic Episodes:

- High energy levels
- Hedonistic mood
- Heightened sex drive
- Irritability
- Racing thoughts
- Unrealistic optimism

Characteristics of Bipolar Type 2 Depressive Episodes:

- Low energy levels
- Sleep disturbance
- Anxiety
- Unrealistic pessimism
- Isolation from people
- Negative thoughts
- Thoughts of suicide or death

- Irritability
- Loss of interest in activities they usually enjoy

Who is at risk of developing bipolar type 2 disorders?

Unfortunately, nearly everyone can be susceptible to this particular mental illness. In fact, in the USA alone, 6 million people (2.5% of the population) suffer from type 2 bipolar.

Generally, sufferers tend to see symptoms arrear in their teens or early 20's, which usually develops further before they reach 50. You are also more susceptible if you have a family member who has previously received treatment in some form or another for either a bipolar disorder or depressive disorder in the past.

Chapter 2
Causes of Bipolar Type 2

Even though medical professionals have carried out a great deal of research into Bipolar Disorder, they still do not completely understand what causes it. However, they have gained a better understanding of the bipolar spectrum especially in relation to the elated highs of mania as well as the lows of depression. In addition, it has helped them to better understand the mood states of people suffering from Bipolar Type 2 between these episodes.

What medical experts are sure of is this disorder runs in families and certain genetic components appear in sufferers. Many also suggest that our environment and lifestyles can have an affect on people developing this condition and its severity. Furthermore, certain events in our lives, which are extremely stressful, can make treating this disorder more difficult as can substance abuse.

Before we look further into what medical professionals claim to be the causes of bipolar, let's briefly look at the bipolar spectrum.

What Is the Bipolar Spectrum?

Bipolar spectrum is a concept, which observes many people with depression, substance abuse and other conditions that have symptoms similar to those of a person suffering from a bipolar disorder.

Under this concept, any people with these conditions, class as being under the "bipolar spectrum", yet do not actually qualify as actually suffering from bipolar. Even though many psychiatrists find the concept useful it's not actually being used much in helping to treat patients.

Possible Causes of Bipolar Type 2:

- **Chemical Imbalance in the Brain**

It is believed by some medical experts that an underlying cause for bipolar is an imbalance of chemicals in the brain (neurotransmitters).

There are three chemicals in the brain, which are involved in helping the body and brain function properly. These are: norepinephrine, (noradrenaline), serotonin and dopamine.

There is a clear link between the brain not producing enough serotonin or norepinephrine and mood disorders such as bipolar and depression. If on the other hand dopamine levels are affected then this can interfere with the brain pleasure receptacles, which can lead to conditions such as schizophrenia or psychosis.

Schizophrenia and psychosis are mental disorders, which cause our thought patterns and behaviours to come erratic as our reality distorts.

- **Genetics**

In recent years, there have been a number of studies carried out on patients and families with bipolar. Results from these clearly show that bipolar does in fact run in families especially in the case of twins.

In many of the identical twin studies carried out concerning bipolar, the statistical data was able to conclude that if one of the twins had bipolar, the other one has between 40 to 70% chance of developing bipolar too.

A further study carried out by John Hopkins University determined that bipolar type 2 was the most common disorder to run in families.

- **Lifestyle & Environment**

As well as there being a genetic link to developing bipolar type 2 it is also said that children who are raised in households where erratic behaviour is prevalent or substance abuse is rife then children are more susceptible to developing bipolar type 2 disorder.

Although not all children who have a parent with bipolar disorder will develop this condition, many will develop other forms of psychiatric disorders such as major depression, ADHA and substance abuse.

It is also believed that certain environmental stressors may be what causes a bipolar episode to be triggered, especially those who are genetically predisposed to developing this disorder.

- **Parental Age**

In a study carried out in September 2008 and published in an issue of the Archive of Psychiatry, suggested that children whose fathers were a lot older when they were born are at risk of developing bipolar disorder1.

Other studies have also shown similar results regarding older fathers and bipolar. Results also show that those children are at risk of developing other conditions such as autism and schizophrenia.

Researchers have found that more often than not a child born to a father in their mid 50's or older have a 37% chance of developing bipolar compared to children born to fathers in their early 20's.

Chapter 3
Symptoms of Bipolar Type 2

The symptoms of bipolar type 2 will vary dependant on the sufferer. In some cases, it is depression, which seems to cause the most problems and in others, it is the manic side.

Furthermore, some will suffer from both sets of symptoms of hypomania and depression at the same time. This is what we refer to as a mixed episode.

Symptoms of a hypomanic episode:

- Euphoria
- Inflated self esteem
- Poor Judgement
- Quicker speech
- Racing thoughts
- Aggressive towards others
- They feel agitated or irritated by things
- They have a lot more energy, so do lots more physical activities
- They take risks – Such as spending lots of money or driving too fast
- Their sex drive may increase
- They do not require as much sleep
- They become distracted very easily
- They may drink more or use drugs and won't be concerned about the effects
- They may miss work or school a lot more
- They start to have delusions or they develop psychosis (a break from knowing what is real)
- They do not perform as well at work or school

Symptoms of a depressive episode:

- Intense feelings of sadness

- Intense feelings of hopelessness
- They start to develop suicidal thoughts or behaviors
- Their levels of anxiety start to increase
- They feel guilty
- They have problems sleeping (either they do not get enough sleep or they sleep too much)
- Their appetite may increase or diminish
- They suffer from fatigue
- They start to lose interest in activities they used to enjoy
- They have problems concentrating on things
- They feel irritable a lot of the time
- They start to suffer from chronic pain but are not sure what is causing it
- They may be absent from work or school more frequently
- Their levels of performance at work or school begin to subside

Other symptoms of bipolar type 2:

- **Mood changes relating to the seasons**

Just like the condition SAD (Seasonal Affective Disorder), there are some people diagnosed with bipolar disorders whose moods change according to the seasons. During the spring and summer months many experience hypomanic episodes and in winter and fall they suffer depressive ones.

However, you should be aware, that is not always the case in many bipolar sufferers, their moods can change at any time.

- **Rapid cycling**

This symptom does not happen to all bipolar type 2 sufferers but it does happen. Rapid cycling is as it sounds; their moods change very rapidly from one to the next.

Generally, for a person to class as suffering from rapid cycling they have to suffer from four or more mood swings in any given year.

The shift in moods also needs to occur much faster, in many cases they can happen within a few hours or days.

- **Psychosis**

For a person to receive a diagnosis of psychosis can only happen when their episodes of either depression or mania are so severe they become detached from reality. Symptoms of psychosis are delusions and hallucinations.

When Should You Seek Medical Advice

If you are experiencing any of the symptoms described in the last few chapters then you should seek medical assistance ASAP.

What you need to understand is without the right kind of treatment; your bipolar disorder is not going to get any better on its own. By seeking assistance from a medical health professional, which has experience in treating this kind of condition, mean you will be able to take control over your illness.

Unfortunately, many never receive any treatment for their condition. Even when they experience severe mood swings, they still do not realize what a dramatic effect it has over their emotional wellbeing. Not only does it disrupt their lives but of those around them also. Many people enjoy the feelings of euphoria but what you need to remember is, a depressive state will follow your euphoric state.

It is also important to always keep contact with your doctor and mental health team long after your diagnosis.

Chapter 4
How is Bipolar Disorder Diagnosed?

Diagnosing Bipolar Type 2 disorder can be very difficult because it is often very difficult to detect. In some cases, people who have suffered with this illness have had to wait 10 years or more before medical professionals have been able to confirm their diagnosis.

The reason why it can take so long to diagnose someone having this illness is down to this conditions dual nature. When someone is feeling hypomanic, (full of energy and upbeat) they seldom choose to seek treatment.

Yet, in many cases they will often look for treatment when they start to have one of their depressive episodes.

Of course, when they do seek treatment they only discuss how they are feeling at that particular time. In turn, this means they receive the misdiagnosis of suffering from depression rather than from a bipolar disorder.

Another reason why doctors often find it hard to determine if a patient is suffering from bipolar disorder or not is because this particular illness shares many of the signs and symptoms associated with other types of psychiatric illnesses. The most common ones being: anxiety disorders, schizophrenia and ADHD.

At this current time, there are no laboratory tests, to detect whether a person is suffering from bipolar. However, by answering certain questions, a doctor is able to determine if this is the case. The questions they use form a questionnaire known as the MDQ (Mood Disorder Questionnaire).

MDQ is more of a checklist, which helps mental health professionals identify if the symptoms you display are in fact bipolar or another mental health disorder.

However, there are now similar questionnaires online but they are nowhere near as accurate as going to see a proper professional.

So how do mental health professionals determine if you have bipolar or not?

They do this by conducting a series of examinations:

- **A Complete Psychiatric History Examination**

This examination requires you to detail your full symptoms you are suffering, not just now but in the past.

They will also need to know of any members of your family, including grandparents, aunts and uncles, who either have displayed the symptoms of a mental health disorder or have received treatment for such.

As we have mentioned before, they need to know this because bipolar type 2 disorder runs in families, therefore if anyone in your family has received a diagnosis of having such then the likelihood of you having it too is much higher.

- **A Complete Medical and Physical History Examination**

They will look at your medical and physical history so they can determine whether another underlying illness could be the cause of your symptoms, which are associated with bipolar type 2.

These could be: diabetes, epilepsy, a salt imbalance or a problematic thyroid gland. They also need to rule out any head injuries, brain tumours, lupus or multiple sclerosis.

Chapter 5
How is Bipolar Type 2 Treated?

There are a number of treatments available for bipolar type 2 sufferers, namely medication, counselling or a combination of both.

Since this illness is a result of a chemical imbalance in the brain then your mental health team will prescribe you with medication, which helps to even this out and stabilize your moods.

As with most medications, there are certain side effects. At first, you may not like the way you feel whilst taking them, which is why many people find it difficult to stick with their medication. It is also important you attend these counselling sessions, which will support and encourage you along the way.

When you attend sessions with a counsellor, psychologist or psychotherapist you learn your illness is just like any other illness and can be treated as such. They also teach you to recognize the symptoms of a manic or depressive episode so you can use certain techniques to help alleviate stress and the severity of your symptoms.

Your mental health team will also help you to identify situations or things in your life, which could trigger episodes and how you can avoid them.

It is a good idea that you attend these sessions with your family. By getting them involved in your therapy sessions, they will learn about the nature of your illness and how they can learn ways to accept it and cope better with it.

The more support and encouragement you receive from those around you will help you to manage your illness much better.

There is a wide variety of medications available to bipolar type 2 sufferers:

- **Mood Stabilizers**
  - *Lithium*

Although this is a simple metal, many find it to be highly effective in controlling a persons mood swings. Its use in the treatment of bipolar has been around for centuries. However, it may be several weeks before you will see any positive effects. It is also highly important you attend regular check-ups to ensure the levels of lithium in your blood stream do reach too high.

  - *Depakote*

Depakote's normal use is for epileptics and controls and prevents seizures. However, it is also very effective at levelling people's moods. Unlike lithium, this drug works quickly so you can see result much faster.

Other forms of anti seizure medication your mental health team may prescribe to you are: Topamax, Tegretol, Neurontin, Gabitril or Trileptal.

  - *Lamictal*

This medication works well on adults who suffer from any "type" of bipolar disorder. It helps to delay bouts of depression, hypomania as well as mixed episodes.

- **Antipsychotics**

A medical professional will only prescribe this medication to people who suffer from severe manic episodes. Not only do the help relieve the symptoms of a manic episode but also prevents them from occurring. The mains ones prescribed are: Abilify, Seroquel, Zyprexa and Risperdal.

- **Benzodiazepines**

More often referred to as tranquilizers these types of medications are only prescribed to patients on a short-term basis in order to help control the more acute symptoms associated with a hypomanic episode.

The most commonly prescribed forms of this medication include Xanax, Ativan and Valium.

- **Antidepressants**

Although some mental health professionals may choose to prescribe antidepressants such as Zoloft, Paxil or Prozac for patients with any form of bipolar disorder they do so in very limited amounts, the reason for this being is they can actually trigger someone to have a manic episode.

In addition, mental health professionals will tend only to prescribe such medication if they find the previous medications described are not helping to bring the symptoms of this illness under control.

Therapy

As well as medication, there are certain types of therapy your mental health team will advise you to attend. These could be:

- **CBT (Cognitive Behavioral Therapy)**

This is the most common type of therapy available to bipolar type 2 sufferers. Through this form of therapy, you will learn to appraise and interpret events, which prove stressful in your life. If you cannot take control, over these events then of course your symptoms exasperate and as a result, you will find keeping them under control a lot more difficult.

With CBT, you will find there are certain methods your therapist will teach you to use. Through these methods, you learn how to become aware of your thought patterns and how you think in a distorted manner so you can then examine the reasons for those thoughts. Then you will learn how to perform certain tests yourself, so you can see them in a different light.

Overtime as a person undergoing CBT you will find they can help to reduce the negative impact this illness has on your life by learning to identify and correct those thoughts, which are leading you to come up with more harmful conclusions.

As part of this therapy, you will be required to write down any thoughts you may be having at the time of an episode and what caused them in the first place. By writing down what you are experiencing, will help you to examine what is happening therefore, you can form a more informed decision about how to deal with them. When you use such strategies, over time you will begin to see your mood swings reduce.

- **FFT (Family Focused Therapy)**

FFT is in a fact, a hybrid of two forms of therapy (psycho-education combined with a form of family therapy). Through the psycho-education part of the therapy, you and your family will see the true nature of your illness for what it is.

Whilst the family part pays more attention to the dynamics of your family and your relationship with your family in order for you, and them, to understand how these can contribute to making your condition worse or better.

From the outset, FFT therapy helps to provide you and your family with a much deeper appreciation of the way the family system, along with its complicated web of relationships, can help to either support your condition or exacerbate it.

Through attending sessions with an FFT therapist, you will work on identifying any difficulties or conflicts within your family, which could be contributing to not only the stress you are feeling but how they are feeling as well. Then once you can identify these, the therapist will help you and your family work on ways to resolve such conflicts and difficulties in the future.

Your FFT therapist will help you and your family to work on ways in which you are all aware of what is happening. This in turn will help you to bring under control any emotions you or they are expressing which could make your illness much worse.

- **IPSRT (Interpersonal and Social Rhythm Therapy)**

This form of therapy looks at using techniques based upon observations relating to disturbances in the body's rhythm, which can lead to mood disturbances.

The techniques often used in this form of therapy are the ones that aim to stabilize the body's rhythm once again. For example, techniques, which will help you to sleep, better.

Patients who are able to establish the right sort of sleeping schedule tend to find their bipolar symptoms reduce.

As part of this therapy, you will be required to keep a mood chart so you and your therapist can monitor your mood states on a daily basis in relation to what you are doing. As part of this chart, you not only record what you are doing on a daily basis, such as when you will sleep, but also what you eat and what activities you are involved in.

Furthermore, as part of this you are required to keep track of interaction with others as well including notes of any conflicts that arise or things, which cause your stress levels to increase.

As your therapist looks through the information, they can then start to establish routines with you, which will help you to become more stable. In addition, they will also help you to identify any events or interactions, which may cause your bodies rhythm to become unbalanced once more so you will know when to avoid these.

Quite a number of people who have undergone this form of therapy have found it very effective in helping to prevent episodes occurring in the future.

Chapter 6
Prognosis For Bipolar Type 2 Sufferers?

There is evidence to suggest that bipolar type 2 is more of a chronic course of illness than bipolar type 1. Certainly, evidence now shows this constant and pervasive form of illness leads to an increased risk of suicidal tendencies.

Furthermore, the time between hypomanic and depressive episodes tends to be much shorter than it is for those suffering from Bipolar Type 1.

If left untreated then there is every chance, you will spend a great deal of your life feeling unwell. Most of these feelings will stem from you feeling depressed quite a lot of the time.

Even though the symptoms tend to be much more severe, there is no evidence to show that the risk of relapse, whilst you are being treated, will be any greater than if you were suffering from bipolar type 1.

In fact, 60% of people who suffer with bipolar type 2 only tend to have another episode within four years of the initial one.

There are some cases where patients tend to be symptomatic half the time, meaning that they either suffer full on episodes or they suffer from symptoms that fall just below what is considered to be the threshold for a full blown episode.

However, the prognosis is only good if patients are willing to take medication long term and undergo therapy on a long-term basis. If they do, they will find this not only helps them to keep their symptoms under control, but will also help to reduce or even prevent a relapse from occurring.

In addition, even with the right form of treatment you will not receive the benefits if you are not willing to take some responsibility for your illness yourself.

What we mean by assuming responsibility for your illness is, you must accept the diagnosis given, take the medication your mental health professional has prescribed and seek help when it is needed, not only now but also in to the future.

Chapter 7
How to Deal With Bipolar Type 2

It does not matter whether you received your diagnosis recently or in the past, and are sticking with your treatment, there are certain things that you can do yourself to help deal with your condition.

1. Take ownership of your condition.

The first thing you need to remember is it's not your fault you have this condition. Once you realize this, you can start to take control over the situation. The best way to do this is by following your treatment regime created for you by your mental health team. It is also crucial you lead a healthier lifestyle.

2. Take the medication as prescribed to you.

No matter what else you do, you must take your medication "exactly" the way your mental health team told you to take it. This must do this on a daily basis. If you think it is okay to only take it when you are feeling depressed or manic then think again.

If you do not take them regularly, you will find missing even one day of your medication could exacerbate your condition further and make the symptoms feel much more severe.

Word of Warning! If you notice you start to feel ill whilst taking your medication, then speak with your mental health team as soon as possible. It could be that your meds need to be either changes or the amount reduced or increased. What you should **NEVER** do is stop taking them; otherwise, this could have serious consequences to your condition.

3. Eliminate alcohol from your diet.

It is easy to hit the bottle when you are feeling a little low but because you suffer from bipolar, it is important that you do not. Just one glass of wine could seriously affect how your medication works. As alcohol mixes with your medication, you could suffer some severe side effects such as seizures and liver damage. Besides, it also influences greatly on your mood swings.

4. Get plenty of sleep.

Ideally, you should be looking to have at least seven to eight hours of sleep each night. Otherwise, lack of sleep can put your moods discordant.

5. Avoid stimulants

The stimulants you should avoid are nicotine and caffeine. All stimulants especially these have quite an effect on moods. They also effect sleep, which means you'll struggle to get your seven to eight hours a night. You also need to cut out any energy drinks that you may consume, because while they may give you a short boost of energy when feeling tired, it is short lived.

6. Establish a healthy routine

The right sort of routine will help to keep your stress levels down which in turn will help to keep your mood levels on a more even keel. As well as eating a healthy well balanced diet you should be aiming to do some exercise on a daily basis.

If you are having trouble developing a routine for yourself then speak with your mental health team who should be able to put you in contact with a therapist who has experience in IPSRT.

7. Avoid triggers and stressors

It is important you not only avoid people but also situations, which cause your stress levels to rise. If you find certain situation or people, agitate you, then try to walk away as soon as possible, if you do not then the likelihood is the situation or person could trigger an episode.

8. Educate yourself

The more you know about your illness the more able you are to take control over it. Reading books like these will help and there are many places online, where you can find information regarding your condition. There are also many support groups around, which can help you to understand what you are going through.

9. Get help!

As well as your mental health team, make sure you enlist the support of your friends and family. The bigger your support networks the better chance you have of overcoming this condition. It is also important that if someone offers to help, make sure you explain clearly, what you want from him or her.

The tips above may sound pretty simple and easy to do but when you are in the throws of a depressive episode, a lot of them will seem like climbing Mount Everest. Just remember, help is there if you need it and don't hesitate to contact your mental health team, who will be more than willing to help you.

Chapter 8
How to Overcome Bipolar Type 2

If you want to overcome Bipolar Type 2 you first need to understand that this is an illness you will have to live with for the rest of your life. There has been lots of research into bipolar but there is still no cure for it. However, the treatments now in use for bipolar, do help to alleviate or prevent the symptoms associated with it.

As well as working with your mental health team, there are things you can do for yourself to help ease your condition. Many self-help methods and techniques can work wonderfully when combined with what your health care team provides to you.

In the book written by Dr Wes Burgess called "The Bipolar Handbook" he explains that 10 to 30% of symptoms associated with this illness can be addressed if you are willing to pay close attention to your lifestyle and make necessary positive changes to it.

<u>So let's look at these:</u>

- It is important you learn to identify the things, which triggers an episode occurring. This is important, because if you are able see when one is about to take place then you can actually take steps to help prevent it from becoming a full blown one. For example if you find attending certain events such as a birthday party triggers an episode then of course it may be worth considering not attending any in the future.

- It is important you take the medication as prescribed by your doctor. This is because they calculate the dosage to base on the severity of your condition but also on how much you weigh.

  However, if you start to suffer from any unwanted side effects or you find that you are not able to tolerate the drug prescribed, tell your doctor immediately. You should never just stop taking your medication!

- You should never miss appointments with your doctor or therapist. It makes it much harder for your mental health team to find out how well you are or are not doing if you miss them. It will also be difficult for them to determine if they need to adjust your medication.
  Keeping appointments will be the best way to ensure your medical team are able to help you any way they can. If you find it hard to keep track of appointments then keep a diary and make a point to look at it every morning.
- It is important you stick to the same routine every day. Although it may take you some time to get your routine in order, it is worth it. You need to make sure you do the same thing every day at the same time as this will help you to get your routine established a lot more quickly.
  The kinds of things you should be doing are: to take your medication at the same time each day, to go to bed at the same time each night and make sure you wake up at the same time each morning.
  If you establish some kind of routine from the outset then it will make managing your life on a daily basis a lot easier. Although you won't see any benefit from doing so initially, over time you will start to see it does help to make things a lot more stable for your and so the risk of your moods fluctuating is greatly reduced.
- It is important to exercise on a regular basis. Ideally, you should be looking to exercise four to five times a week.
  However, because your moods tend to change quite a bit, you may find it difficult sometimes to be motivated into any kind of exercise. Yet even when in a depressive state you will find going for a short walk can help to alleviate some of the symptoms and feelings associated with this illness.
- Have a shower every day, as this will then help you to eliminate any negative thoughts or feelings you may have. Just stand under the shower and let everything flow away with the water. Even when depressed you may think

30

having a shower will not help you any, but you may be surprised at what a difference it can make.

- If you really want to deal with your illness more effectively then you should keep a journal. Through this, you will be able to ensure you keep your appointments with your medical team and learn more about what causes your episodes.

  In addition, it allows you to then share important information with your doctor or therapist, which they may find useful in helping to treat your illness more effectively.

- Take up an activity, which you enjoy and keeps you busy. Remember the aim of taking up such activities is to help prevent any negative thoughts from being able to take control over your life.

  Even if you only spend 30 minutes to an hour each day on this activity, it really can prove beneficial to you. If you can join some sort of group where you are required to interact with others, especially choose groups, which have been specifically set up for those suffering from bipolar disorder.

Chapter 9
Importance of a Healthy Diet to a Bipolar Type 2 Sufferer

Previously in this book, I have discussed the importance of a healthy lifestyle and diet but now I want to take a step further and look at why and how you can do that.

Ok so we are not rewriting history here. Everyone knows how important a good healthy diet is to your overall health and wellbeing. However, you will be surprised to know how little people realize the impact diet has on your mental health.

Results from studies suggest that following a very simple bipolar diet and nutrition plan can help you to deal with your condition better.

In fact, in one study carried out by Evanne Constantine and Wesley Freeman Smith of Lewisham Counselling and Counsellor Associates, suggest there is a strong link between your nutritional intake and your condition. If you were to make changes to your diet, which include taking certain vitamins, specifically, Magnesium, Vitamin B and Omega 3, you will find these help to minimize the intensity and frequency of your episodes. In addition, if you were to reduce your intake of foods containing caffeine and sugar the treatment for your condition will be more effective.

Is following a specific diet really going to help?

The answer is of course, yes! Dr Goodwin and Dr Jamison found, in their study, that people who suffered from bipolar type 2 also suffered from hypoglycaemia. What this means is, after each meal you eat, your blood sugar levels will drop within 1 to 3 hours. This then results in symptoms such as depression, irritability, fatigue, difficulty concentrating and panic attacks.

Yet, if you were to make changes by starting to eat foods, which helps to stabilize your insulin levels within your body, you can stabilize your blood sugar levels in the process.

Not only will you start to see your moods improve, you reduce the risk of putting on weight. Many people who suffer with bipolar type 2 begin to put on weight because of the medication they need to take. Weight gain causes major medical conditions such as heart disease, diabetes and strokes. In fact, people suffering with bipolar are twice as likely to die from those medical conditions than those who do not.

Therefore, it is important you speak to your doctor or mental health professional to come up with a personalized diet and nutritional plan, which suits your basic needs.

The plan you come up with should be well balanced and be primarily plant based. You also need to make sure you include foods from each food group.

Chapter 10
What's Involved?

In the last 10 years, more people who suffer with bipolar type 2 are turning to dietary therapy programs to help them manage their condition better. Although dietary therapy programs do help, it is important to use them in conjunction with other forms of treatment. Do not use them as an alternative. If you also want to get the best out of your dietary program, you should consult with your doctor or mental health professional to help you create a plan, which is best suited to you and your needs.

It is important to remember this type of diet is to provide you with nutritional support as well as improving your emotional wellbeing. There are certain foods and nutrients when included in your diet not only helps to improve brain function but helps to reduce the severity of certain symptoms associated with bipolar.

What should you include in your diet?

1. Nutrients

Whether suffering with bipolar or not, nutrients are an important element to a healthy lifestyle. However, as a bipolar type 2 you need to place emphasis on making sure you get sufficient amounts of vitamins A and D as well as complex carbohydrates. Complex carbs help to keep your blood sugar levels balanced and provide you with some positive energy.

You also need to include proteins. For adults with bipolar type 2, their daily intake of protein is 50 mg. For children it should be a least 25 mg.

2. Healthy Foods

Healthy foods are a staple part of any dietary therapy program. Studies show, eating fresh healthy foods rather than taking supplements can prove more effective to those suffering with bipolar.

Chapter 11
Creating the Right Plan

As we have discussed previously, your condition is characterized by alternating periods of hypomania and depression. Some of the symptoms you will suffer from during these times include disturbance to your sleeping patterns, being very irritable, having difficulty concentrating and sometimes loss of inhibitions. By following the right sort of diet, you can manage these symptoms more effectively.

If you follow the simple steps below, with the advice of your doctor on creating a diet and nutritional plan for you, you can help to combat your symptoms.

Step 1

It is important to include foods high in protein, healthy fats and plenty of vegetables and whole grains. Not only will the amino acids in protein help to combat feelings of depression but also help to keeping your blood sugar levels normal. The healthy fats you find in fish, olive oil and flaxseed oil not only help for better brain functioning but also your nervous system.

Step 2

Reduce your intake of sugar, caffeine and alcohol. The problem with these is they stimulate your body and can worsen symptoms associated with bipolar disorder.

The biggest problem with sugar, including those found in alcohol, is they fluctuate your blood sugar levels dramatically, which can make your mood swings more excessive. Alcohol may make you feel fine for a while but can act as a depressant and so can exacerbate your depressive episodes even more.

Step 3

When you are suffering from a depressive episode, make sure you eat plenty of foods, which boosts your serotonin levels. When people feel depressed, their serotonin levels are usually low, so eating foods that contain these certainly helps with this.

The kinds of foods, which contain serotonin, are plums, avocados, tomatoes, bananas and pineapples. However, if you are suffering with a hypomanic episode then avoid these foods since your serotonin levels will be high already.

Step 4

Include vitamins and minerals such as vitamin B, essential fatty acid DHA, zinc, magnesium and calcium.

Vitamin B and the essential fatty acid DHA help to combat depressive feelings whilst in a depressive episode. Zinc, magnesium and calcium help to make you feel calmer during a manic episode.

Things to be aware of

Before you make any changes to your diet, you must first speak with your mental health team to determine whether you may be allergic to any foods. The last thing you want is find you are allergic to something, which can worsen your symptoms.

It may also be a good idea in the beginning to keep a food diary, noting down every thing you have eaten or drank and how it made you feel afterwards. This will help you to identify any foods or drinks, which could trigger a hypomanic or depressive episode.

Chapter 12
What Should You Include In Your Diet Plan?

It is important to make sure you include these essential vitamins, minerals and foods into your diet plan:

1. Omega 3 Fatty Acids

In clinical trials carried out by the University of Maryland Medical Center, they discovered that people who ate fatty fish twice a week experienced decreased feelings of depression. If you do not include omega 3 fatty acids into your diet, you will find the nerves in your brain are not able to communicate effectively which leads to increase feelings of depression.

Try to make sure you consume 3 ounces of fatty fish such as, mackerel, salmon, sardines or tuna twice a week. You can also find omega 3 in other foods such as, walnuts, canola oil and flax seed.

2. Fruits and Vegetables

By including plenty of fresh fruit and veg in your diet, you are providing your body with a large number of very helpful nutrients that support and improve your overall wellness.

In an article published in the New York Times in December 2009, suggested a diet rich in these foods, not only help to elevate symptoms of bipolar type 2 but help to combat weight issues too.

Controlling weight is an issue if you are taking prescription medication given to you by your mental health professional. Most medication for bipolar sufferers on the market today makes you gain weight. That is why it is important to control this weight gain by eating healthy.

3. Whole Grains

You will find foods such as pasta; cereals and whole grain breads contain fiber and water. These help to promote healthy blood sugar levels. If you do not create stability in your sugar levels then you'll not only find your physical energy levels will fluctuate but that of your moods too. Try to cut out white bread and sugar cereals and replace them with the whole grain variety.

4. Lean Proteins

Foods, which contain lean proteins, include poultry (chicken and turkey), fish, legumes (beans and peas) and low fat dairy products. One of the most important of these is vitamin B as this helps to regulate your mood swings better.

It's key to include either 3 ounces of fish or poultry in each meal along with ½ cup of beans or peas or 1 cup of low fat dairy food.

Recommended Resources

Downloaded & Read My Book?
Please Leave Your Comments Now!
I Appreciate It Very Much
http://www.amazon.com/dp/B008A8TRHG

Other Kindle Books In The Bipolar Series

Please visit my author page now

http://amazon.com/author/ultimatesurvivorguides